Marsupials

LEVEL 10

Teaching Tips

White Level 10

This book focuses on developing reading independence, fluency, and comprehension.

Before Reading

- Ask readers what they think the book will be about based on the title. Have them support their answer.

Read the Book

- Encourage readers to read silently on their own.
- As readers encounter unfamiliar words, ask them to look for context clues to see if they can figure out what the words mean. Encourage them to locate boldfaced words in the glossary and ask questions to clarify the meaning of new vocabulary.
- Allow readers time to absorb the text and think about each chapter.
- Ask readers to write down any questions they have about the book's content.

After Reading

- Ask readers to summarize the book.
- Encourage them to point out anything they did not understand and ask questions.
- Ask readers to review the questions on page 23. Have them go back through the book to find answers. Have them write their answers on a separate sheet of paper.

© 2024 Booklife Publishing
This edition is published by arrangement with Booklife Publishing.

North American adaptations © 2024 Jump!
5357 Penn Avenue South
Minneapolis, MN 55419
www.jumplibrary.com

Library of Congress Cataloging-in-Publication Data is available at www.loc.gov or upon request from the publisher.

ISBN: 979-8-88524-811-2 (hardcover)
ISBN: 979-8-88524-812-9 (paperback)
ISBN: 979-8-88524-813-6 (ebook)

Photo Credits

Images are courtesy of Shutterstock.com. With thanks to Getty Images, Thinkstock Photo and iStockphoto. Cover – Smileus. p4–5 – Alberto Gomez Pando Baena, Andrii Slonchak. p6–7 -EA Given, Chris Howey. p8–9 – tinokoloski, Anom Harya. p10–11 – rickyd, TM picture. p12–13 – Susan Flashman. p14–15 –slowmotiongli, Richard A Wall. p16–17 - Phillip Minnis, Maik Boenig. p18–19 - Andras Deak, BMJ. p20–21 - Phillip W. Kirkland, Manon van Os.

Table of Contents

What Is a Marsupial?

Marsupials are warm-blooded **mammals** that produce milk for their young. Most marsupials have a pouch. Young marsupials live in the pouch until they are big enough to explore outside. Most marsupials live in Australia, but a few **species** live in Central and South America.

Pouch

There are more than 300 species of marsupials in the world. Although marsupials are similar to each other, they have each adapted differently for their habitats. Some marsupials live high up in the trees and others live in burrows under the ground. The largest marsupial in the world is the red kangaroo.

Red kangaroo

Body Parts

Marsupials come in all shapes and sizes, and although they are all marsupials, they can sometimes look quite different from each other. They are similar to other types of mammals, but most marsupials are born very early and feed on their mother's milk from inside the pouch.

Baby quokka

Tail

Many marsupials have long, strong tails. Some marsupials, such as kangaroos and wallabies, use their tails for balance as they jump. They can also use them to push themselves forward, like a third leg. The tail is so strong that it can hold the kangaroo's body weight.

Pouches

Nearly all female marsupials have a pouch. The pouch is a fold of skin. A newborn baby crawls inside when it is very tiny. It stays there for around eight months and drinks its mother's milk. It stays safe and warm.

Unlike kangaroos, wombat pouches open at the rear.

Patagia

Some marsupials live high up in the forest trees. They must travel from tree to tree to find food and escape from **predators**. Some trees are very far apart, so these marsupials **evolved** to grow special pieces of skin called patagia. The patagia act like wings and allow the animals to glide.

Patagia

Moving Around

Marsupials move around in different ways depending on their habitat. Marsupials that only live in trees, such as sugar gliders and koalas, are called arboreal marsupials and are very good at holding onto tree branches. Ones that live on the land, such as kangaroos and wombats, are known as terrestrial marsupials.

Koala

Most terrestrial marsupials use four legs to move across the ground. Kangaroos have two legs and two arms. They jump forward by using both feet at the same time. They can cover more than 23 feet in one jump and can hop nearly seven feet up in the air.

Red kangaroo

Eating

Marsupials have different teeth depending on whether they eat other animals, plants, or both. Tasmanian devils eat mostly snakes, birds, insects, and fish. They also eat dead animal carcasses, called carrion. Tasmanian devils have long canine teeth to tear off the meat easily.

Tasmanian devil

The tiger quoll is a predator that hunts small animals such as birds, rats, possums, and rabbits. Tiger quolls are also scavengers. This means that they eat the meat of animals that other predators have already killed. Quolls are also the **prey** of larger predators such as foxes, cats, and Tasmanian devils.

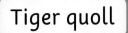

Tiger quoll

Habitats

Habitats are the homes of living things. They provide food and shelter for the plants and animals that live in them. Kangaroos and wallabies live in grasslands, while marsupial moles burrow underground. Marsupial mice live on the forest floor, and gliding possums live in nests high up in the trees.

Kowari

The koala's favorite food is eucalyptus leaves. They spend all of their time eating and sleeping, so they sit in eucalyptus trees where they can easily reach their food and stay safely hidden from predators on the ground.

Adaptation

Many marsupials have adapted to their environments in amazing ways. Adaptations are changes that help an animal survive. Water opossums live in streams and lakes and have useful features for living in water. Their fur is short and doesn't absorb water, and their back feet are webbed, making them good swimmers.

Water opossum habitat

Wombats are very good diggers and do lots of burrowing underground. When they are digging their burrows, they shovel dirt and soil toward their bodies. Wombats have a special adaptation that stops any soil from getting inside their pouch: their pouches open at the rear and face backward.

Life Cycle

The life cycle of an animal is the series of changes it goes through from the start to the end of its life. The life cycle of marsupials is similar to that of other mammals. Just like other mammals, the female marsupials give birth to live young.

A baby marsupial is called a joey. All joeys are born after just a few weeks. Newborn joeys are pink, very small, hairless, blind, and have no ears. They do most of their growing inside their mother's pouch, where they feed on milk.

Amazing Marsupials

Snakes are a big danger to mammals all over the world. They kill their prey by biting and injecting them with **venom**. Virginia opossums are immune to snake venom. This means that they will not be harmed if they are bitten by a snake.

Virginia opossum

Koalas have a very strange diet. They are one of the few animals that can eat the leaves that grow on a eucalyptus tree. To most other animals, these leaves are very poisonous, but the koala's body can break down the leaves.

Koalas have special teeth for eating leaves.

Index

How to Use an Index

An index helps us find information in a book. Each word has a set of page numbers. These page numbers are where you can find information about that word.

Page numbers

Example: balloons 5, 8–10, 19

Important word

This means page 8, page 10, and all the pages in between. Here, it means pages 8, 9, and 10.

Questions

1. What is a baby marsupial called?

2. Where do sugar gliders live?
    a. In trees
    b. On the ground
    c. In lakes and streams

3. What is the favorite food of the koala?

4. Can you use the Table of Contents to find what habitat kangaroos live in?

5. Can you use the Index to find information about a water opossum?

6. Using the Glossary, can you define what a mammal is?

Glossary

evolved:
Gradually changed from one generation to the next.

mammals:
Warm-blooded animals that have hair or fur and usually give birth to live babies. Female mammals produce milk to feed their young.

predators:
Animals that hunt other animals for food.

prey:
Animals that are hunted by other animals for food.

species:
One of the groups into which similar animals and plants are divided.

venom:
Poison produced by some snakes and spiders.